CW00502755

CREATIVE BLOCK

Over 500 Ideas to Ignite Your Imagination

by Lou Harry

RUNNING PRESS

PHILADELPHIA · LONDON

9 8 7 6 5 4 3 2 1
Digit on the right indicates the number of this printing

Library of Congress Control Number: 2004096975

ISBN 0-7624-2280-7

Cover and interior design by Alicia Freile
Edited by August Tarrier
Typography: Bureau Grotesque, Frutiger, and New Caledonia

This book may be ordered by mail from the publisher.
Please include $2.50 for postage and handling.
But try your bookstore first!

Running Press Book Publishers
125 South Twenty-second Street
Philadelphia, Pennsylvania 19103-4399

Visit us on the web!
www.runningpress.com

DEDICATION

When my brother was collecting autographs of baseball players, I decided to write to some authors I was reading and ask for their signatures. This book is dedicated to those writers—including David Gerrold and William F. Nolan— who graciously took the time to write back.

INTRODUCTION

You're stuck.
Blank.
Nothing.

The fingers don't move on the keyboard. The pictures don't appear in your mind. The ideas that you need just won't formulate.

Whether you are a marketing exec who has to come up with a brilliant presentation by tomorrow, a novelist stuck in a plot corner, an engineer who needs to figure out a creative solution to a challenging technical problem, or a Sunday school teacher who needs to come up with a crafts project, you know what it's like to be ready to create but not have the fuel to move.

Creative Block strikes when we expect it and when we don't. It strikes when we are trying to launch a project and when we are desperately trying to complete one. It strikes when we are alone with pen and paper and it strikes when there's a room full of performers looking to you for guidance.

Okay, you try to tell yourself, it's not that serious. It's not like a surgeon suddenly forgetting how to operate or a police officer blanking on the law.

But that doesn't help.

Perhaps there is some consolation in the fact that Creative Block is something that happens to many, many people. But then again, consolation doesn't get the job done.

What does?

In the following pages, you'll find hundreds of answers to that question. On every page, you'll find something designed to get your creative juices flowing. Some are very general, applicable to all creative endeavors. Others will apply more directly to some disciplines than to others. When you see the word "imagine," feel free to replace it with "write about," "dance," "paint," or anything else that works for you.

While most pages offer ideas and exercises, there are a number of recurring concepts.

Inside, you'll find:

- "Spark" Words: Single words or phrases to foster your imagination.
- "Spark" Quotes: Lines of dialogue to get your inner voices talking.
- "Spark" Settings: When location is what you need to start rolling.
- Explain It: A snapshot of a moment— your task is to use your imagination to fill in the details.
- Get Their Story: Sources to tap for new worlds of ideas.

You'll also find "Expert Advice," featuring creative people whose ideas are key to their livelihoods. Most of them are presenting their advice and experiences here for the first time. Trust them: They've been down the road that, to you, might seem untraveled.

Obviously, this book is not meant to be read from cover to cover, start to finish. It's less like a traditional book and more like the treasure chest that your childhood dentist used to let you dig into after an appointment. Just reach in and pull out an idea.

A couple of words of advice:

• Note that just about any block-removing tool in this book can be abused—there's a fine line between inspiration and distraction. It's crucial to realize when you've crossed that line—when, for instance, you've spent too much time in a hot bath or at the batting cage.

• Remember that no two creative people are the same. Your ideas and approach are uniquely your own. Take advantage of your unique perspective when exercising your creative muscles.

• At the same time, know your audience. Your approach will be—and should be—different depending on whether you are creating for your own satisfaction, trying to please a teacher, attempting to sell books, or shooting for the Pulitzer Prize.

• Above all, know that every creator starts with an empty page, a blank canvas, a lump of clay or some other void.

Let that idea free you rather than intimidate you.

Go.

A battlefield

"Sidetracked"

Imagine the
person it
came from.

The Internet is full of misinformation. Assume, though, that the next piece of junk e-mail you receive contains a pitch that is really true.

"Rural"

poems that only you can write. We are called to give what it is we uniquely have to give. If we refuse the call, the world loses that unique gift forever. You were born to tell the stories that only you can tell."

because our internal critic
or perfectionist becomes too
powerful. You have many pieces
to write. The one you are writing
today doesn't have to be your
greatest masterpiece, it just has
to the one you write today.

"One last thing: Remember
there are songs and stories and

isn't forthcoming," she adds.

"In my experience, inspiration usually strikes within the process. Some people may create only from blissful inspiration, the rest of us mere mortals struggle, wrestle, delight and grapple with the process.

"Remember to be kind to yourself. Many of us get stuck

home from school, turn up the music and dance in the living room, meditate, pray, go to an art gallery, make chocolate-chip cookies and give them away at the office, read, read, read and then read some more."

"I've had people tell me they get stuck because they are waiting for inspiration, and the inspiration her recent best-of collection, *Betty's Diner* (Rounder Records).

"If you are blocked, do some living. Go to a movie, take a short trip, visit a local diner and write down the dialogue you hear, get some crayons and draw a picture, take a knitting class, kiss and hug your kids for no good reason when they come

Expert Advice: Carrie Newcomer, singer/songwriter

"Creating is one of our highest endeavors as humans. We create as we were created. This is a holy and honorable thing," says Carrie Newcomer, a singer/songwriter with nine albums to her credit—from her debut *Visions and Dreams* (Philo Records) to

Make fun of the next
commercial you see.

Turn on the TV.

Recall a time when you learned something for the first time.

"Premature"

Bake something.

"Mutt"

Walk a character into a bar and describe what he or she sees, hears, smells. Is this the first visit? Or a regular stop?

A thousand jokes begin with "A guy walks into a bar."

"Ironic"

Invent someone who rationalizes missing an important meeting.

Where in the world would you go if you had a complimentary ticket anywhere?

Type out
the text of
each.

Go through a magazine
and pick out 10 ads you
think are effective.

"Worthless"

Your neighbor

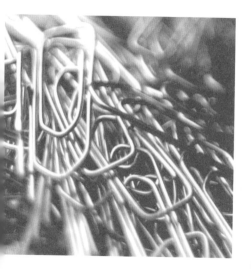

Make a really long
paperclip chain.

Invent a history
for that person or
those people.

Remember the photo that came with the picture frame you purchased?

Reading only these ads, what do you know about the reader?

Ask someone to buy a magazine at random, cut out the ads, and throw away the rest.

Learn as much as you can
about his or her life.

Introduce yourself to a neighbor or co-worker you've never talked to before.

Invent a child who
knows that what
a trusted adult is
telling him is wrong.

"Secret"

Imagine the world from the point of view of your pet.

What about the last kiss?

Much is said of the
first kiss.

A car stuck in traffic

Normally that would be a big failure, but when facing writer's block, it's more like, 'wow, I wrote two pages.'"

was blowing me away, that would make me delay the process more.

"The other thing I do is start off with unambitious goals, like writing two pages in a day.

"When there are no deadlines, that's when I experience it."

So what does he do? "One method is to read other people's scripts. I feel like that gets me in the groove of the format and the structure. You tend to go 'I can do better than that.' It's comforting to read stuff that's not so great. If I read stuff that

or boring. When that happens, you accept that it's like athletics: everyone isn't getting on base, but if some people are, you can win the game. Of course, if you don't get on base the whole season, that would be problematic." It's different when Fink turns his hands to screenplays and television pilots.

something. You had to deliver.
Of course, when you are on a
sitcom staff [Fink also wrote
for *The Drew Carey Show*] there
are days when you feel like the
jokes aren't coming easily or the
story that is being pursued isn't
something that strikes you.
Either you find it implausible

Expert advice: Hugh Fink, television comedy writer

When you write for *Saturday Night Live*, you've got to keep the ideas coming—even if only a small percentage end up on the air. "At *SNL*, you always have to turn stuff in," says Hugh Fink. "There wasn't time to dwell on

. . . especially if you've
never fished before.

Go fishing . . .

They could belong
to you, a character
you are writing about,
your boss, or your
potential audience.

Make a list
of wants.

Use sidewalk chalk
in front of your house
or apartment.

Spend a half hour
in a greenhouse or
garden shop.

Drive to work via
a different route.

Look at things differently.

Sit on the floor
in a corner of
the room.

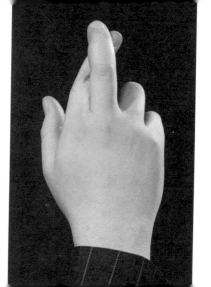

"Lie"

Wake up two hours
earlier tomorrow.

Go to bed two hours earlier than usual tonight.

Let it pour
onto the page.

Write about what
happened yesterday.

Try to recreate an
art project that you
remember from
elementary school.

"Childish"

Take a long shower.

Don't assume you are a day person, a night person, or any other kind of person. If the ideas don't come in the morning, try working late at night instead.

"Wealth"

If you are working on an assigned project—be it a speech, a magazine article or a request for proposal—reread the original instructions.

"Magic"

We are all improvisers in life. We don't know what's going to happen next.

Watch an improvisation team on television or, better yet, live. Watch how they are able to change direction in a scene at the drop of a word.

Don't expect all inspiration to come while staring at a computer screen.

Enter an unusual competition. Try to achieve something no one thought to try to achieve. Books have been written about everything from competing at Scrabble to reading the entire *Encyclopedia Britannica*.

Construct a better ending.

Recall a movie you've seen recently that disappointed you.

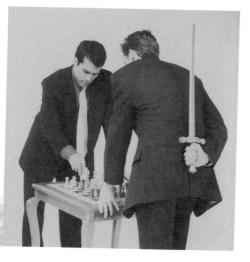

GET THEIR STORY:

Someone you worked
with or work for

"First car"

Write the part of the story, choreograph the sequence of the dance, draft the section of your essay or paint the picture that you know the best—the part that is crying to get out of you. This can ease the delivery of the more difficult passages.

Are you having trouble
with an opening?
Put it aside.

"Cry"

Cast them with real actors.

Imagine that your life
has been turned into
a sitcom. Who are the
six main characters?

The cheap seats

Then check a thesaurus
for 10 similar words to
the ones you first used.

List 10 words to
describe a key element
in your creative task.

Make note of things that were totally at the whim of the architect or artist.

Take an architectural
tour of your city.

Heckle.

Visit a comedy club.

"Nauseating"

Write about how things flowed differently before it struck.

Write about your
creative block.
Write about how
it feels.

Recall the stupidest thing you did when you were younger.

A sibling or old friend
recalls the moment when
you most embarrassed
him or her.

What is the most expensive object you've ever bought? What did you think about as you were buying it? Remember the moments that led up to a major purchase.

(That is, assuming you
aren't 9 years old.)

What would be different
about your day today if
you were 9 years old?

Make something
out of kids'
modeling clay.

Write about a third date.

He's lived a pampered life, is independently wealthy, and can easily afford such luxuries. When words fail him, he goes to Tuscany for a month to play golf. Someday, I hope to be able to have a writer's block like that."

that I'll run out of time to say them, that God, in his peculiar way of doing things, will yank me from this world before I've thrown in my two cents.

"I have a friend who writes for a living who is regularly cursed with writer's block.

early Reagan years, jobs were scarce, so I returned to the road kill. "Since then, it has been etched in my psyche that if I fail as a writer, I would have to return to my road kill job. With an incentive like that, I can't afford writer's block.

"My biggest worry isn't that I'll run out of things to say, but

underappreciated authors who
wanted to make their craft look
harder than it is. I once picked
up road kill for a summer. After
a week on the job, I developed
road kill block. I did all I could
to avoid the task. Phoned in sick,
vomited in the boss's truck,
and spent evenings looking for
another job. But this was in the

past 18 years, 9 books in 11 years, and not once have I fallen silent. I sit at my desk and the words come, sometimes slowly, but they eventually arrive. To be sure, some of my efforts lack a certain sparkle, but I've never missed a deadline.

"Writer's block, I'm coming to believe, was a myth begun by

"Ironically, when asked to talk about writer's block, I'm at a loss for words," says Phil Gulley, a Quaker pastor as well as the author of the best-selling essay collection *Front Porch Tales* and the fictional Harmony series. "Fifty sermons a year for the

Attend a religious service
of a faith that isn't yours.

Rewrite your task as a recipe. What are the necessary ingredients? What are the essentials and what's there to add spice? Outline the procedure. Follow it, step by step.

Make the
problem
simpler

What would the bar's texture be?

If a confection company produced the perfect candy bar, what would it contain?

"Guess what?"

Invent a reason why
someone can't say
something that needs
to be said.

"Reject"

Read the Op-Ed
section of the
New York Times

"Foreign"

Break down the task
into its smallest possible
components.

If you are having
trouble creating,
try un-creating.

And the most selfish
people you know
personally.

List the
nicest people
you know
personally.

"We need
to talk."

"Blast"

idea to say, 'you know what? I'm not going to get anything done right now.' Why not do that, or play guitar, or whatever? If not, I would just look at news on the Internet for hours anyway."

Or he walks away from the computer to play some music. "You hear about foosball and pinball in office buildings as a thing for people to do when they are really stuck. I think that's helpful. Sometimes it's a good

"Sometimes I seek out newspaper articles that I think will piss me off and put fire in my belly. When I do have a block, I just force myself to do it, even if I'm not totally happy with the result. But sometimes you make a great one *because* you have to buckle down and do it."

pressure of deadlines over me every week. On the Internet, I can update whenever I want. On someone else's schedule, I feared I would start to turn out mediocre work."

Still, deadlines do loom and ideas aren't always there. "I don't have any formula or special thing that I do," he says.

cult following. Loyal readers
flock to his website for his latest
off-the-wall creations.

His first step to fighting
creative block is avoiding the
problem completely. "When
I got some public notice with
Get Your War On," says Rees,
"I still didn't aggressively pursue
work because I didn't want the

Expert advice:

David Rees, cartoonist

David Rees's unusual comic strips, collected in the anthologies *Get Your War On* (originally written for *Rolling Stone* magazine) and *My New Fighting Technique Is Unstoppable* (created while working a boring office job), have earned him a

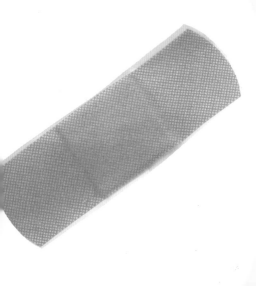

Recall a childhood injury.

$$2 + 2 = 5$$

"Wrong"

Once you have a
terrible version,
improve it.

Consider the task at hand. How would you do it if you didn't care about the quality? If you weren't as bright as you are? If you had no respect for your audience?

"Strike"

A locker room

"Preposterous"

Turn on QVC, the Home Shopping Network, or an equivalent right now. Write down as much information as you can about the object being sold.

"Is that really what
you think of me?"

After
the party

. . . (but only where
no one will worry
about you).

Scream . . .

Try to sing it to a different tune.

Look at the
lyric of a song
you know well.

Inside a tent,
in the woods.

In order to keep
watching, you have to
try to answer—verbally—
every question.

Watch a game show.

Transcribe the
tape at the end
of each day.

Carry a microcassette recorder
for an entire week, using it
whenever you have even the
germ of an idea.

"Vows"

Imagine that person
committing a crime.

Who is the most boring person you know?

A doorway

Create a quiz about
the subject you are
wrestling with.

"Stones"

Make a sundae
with at least one
ingredient you
don't usually use.

For two minutes, talk
out loud to yourself
about every story on
the front page.

Buy a newspaper.

Ask your parents to recall
a memory they never
shared with you.

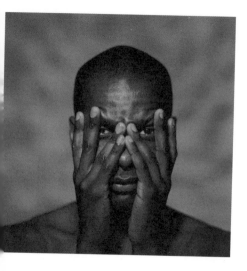

"Regret"

Visit an art museum or gallery. Find a painting that includes at least two people. Imagine the relationship.

Go to a driving range and hit a bucket of balls.

Then destroy all
records of your
venting.

Make fun of the person who gave you the assignment. Say nasty things about him or her. Get it out of your system.

Have you ever hit another person? Whether you have or not, think about the moment just before the decision is made to strike—and the moment after.

Even if no ideas come,
you'll still have gotten
a massage.

Treat yourself
to a massage.

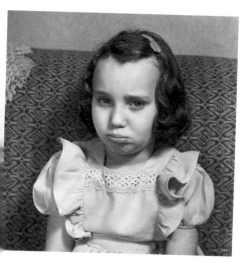

Waiting room

"Ancient"

Try writing an entire story on one, always being aware of how much room you have left (you cannot use more than one!).

Many great ideas
were scribbled on
paper napkins.

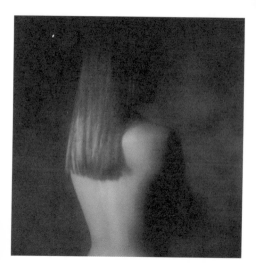

Invent a first encounter between two people who will eventually destroy each other.

Why did you pick
that person? Try to
picture that person
doing the job.

If you could
hire someone
to do this task
for you, who
would it be?

Bounce your idea off them.

Gather a group of kids
as a focus group.

"Prayer"

"Closing time"

When was the last time you just sat on the floor and built something out of LEGOS?

Revert.

"I always quit if I have no ideas, and read," he says, then quotes Winston Churchill, who said, "The further backward you can look, the farther forward you are likely to see. "This works for science fiction especially," he adds. "Not forcing writing but letting the inner landscape lie fallow, does wonders for me."

Expert advice: Gregory Benford, science fiction writer

Sometimes the best solution to creative blockage is not to create at all, according to Gregory Benford, professor at the University of California at Irvine and acclaimed author of such novels as *Beyond Infinity* and *The Martian Race*. On writing:

From that pile, select
three or four images
and tie them together
somehow.

Have a family member or friend take a newspaper that you haven't read and cut out a few photos, not including the captions.

List the last five
pieces of gossip you
heard recently.

"Addiction"

Try yoga.

Who is the person in
real life that you think
is closest to that ideal?

A superhero is usually someone with an extraordinary skill. Think of a skill for a superhero.

A protest march

Take time to watch the movie again or to reread the book, paying close attention to the moment he or she first appears.

Who is your favorite
or most memorable
fictional character?

Describe your favorite teacher.

"Abandoned"

Brainstorm a list of the
worst things someone
might say about your
finished product.

Sometimes what stops creativity is the fear of eventual criticism.

Take a half hour and clear up as many of these as you can. Schedule a half hour every few hours to focus on getting the small things off your plate.

Make a list of small tasks

that are distracting you

from your main project.

Pay particular attention to the "Spoonful of Sugar" sequence.

Watch
Mary Poppins.

Read a famous
speech—in its
entirety.

Everyone knows
"Four score and seven
years ago" but few
know the rest.

Write your rationale
for giving up on it.

Recall the last book you
started reading but
never finished.

"Emergency"

Give a serious read to the magazine that, on the surface, you are the least interested in.

Visit a bookstore or newsstand.

Sometimes, what gets
in the way are too
many choices.

Limit your options.

When was the point in
your life when you felt
the most graceful?

Choreographers magnify,
exaggerate and beautify
how people move.

"Swinger"

Make sure to build
downtime into your
schedule.

Take recess.

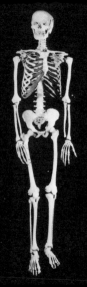

An outline is the skeleton of your work. Some creative people thrive on outlines; others want to make discoveries through the process of writing. Try both ways to see which works best for you.

Read old letters—
if possible, letters
not written by
or to you.

"Something's wrong."

Make lists of things you know about each person who lives there.

Make a chart of your street or the floor of your building.

it anywhere and read about words that connect, words that bring up ideas, words that come from other words. It's a pool where magic is hidden just below the surface. Not a week goes by that I don't use this dumb little trick."

"But there is a little trick I use when I'm absolutely stumped: When I don't have a damn idea, when I don't know what I'm going to say about a subject, when I'm at my most desperate, I sit down and read the thesaurus. Without any plan. I just open

exercise is to look at everything
our competitors do—whatever
our consumer would see when
they look for the same kind of
fulfillment my client offers.
That's the starting point.

Expert advice:

Diane Meier, marketer

"Often I'm in the position of finding a creative center for our clients," says Diane Meier, head of Meier Brands in New York and creative director for such accounts as Neiman Marcus and Maximilian Furs. "My first

Once you've finished, go there and write another description of the same place. This time, treat it in the here-and-now.

Describe—without going there—your favorite room in your house or apartment. Imagine that you haven't been there for 20 years.

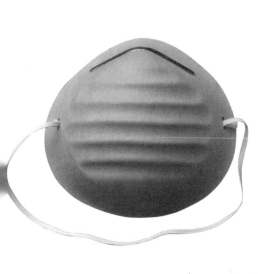

"Bad breath"

Give yourself a reward:
Ten minutes of game-play,
web-surfing or news reading
for every five ideas.
Stick with that plan—no
advances allowed.

Make a commitment not to surf the Internet until you've finished at least one aspect of your project. It's too easy to rationalize a distraction as research.

. . . who can speak, of course.

Your youngest relative . . .

Also, know who you aren't interested in reaching.

Make sure you have a clear idea about whom you are trying to influence or entertain. Find a picture that represents that person or those people.

How would you tell a stranger about the project you are working on?

The creative people in the advertising community have to make a product appealing in just a few words or images.

Watch it.

Ask the clerk at your local video store to recommend a movie that no one seems to be renting.

Ask yourself:

"Who or what will I influence?"

Be the project.

Take five characters and three recurring sets and write synopses for fifteen episodes.

Sitcoms succeed on the basis of their characters and their ability to hold up over many 30-minute (or even less with commercials) episodes.

A jail cell

Time can help separate the
workable ideas from ones
that should be put aside.

Build time in your
schedule for your ideas
to incubate.

What would they have to say?

Imagine four specific people from different backgrounds and of different ages looking at the problem you are facing.

Give yourself a tangible incentive. What is your favorite local restaurant? Don't eat there until your latest project is complete.

Your oldest living relative

"Mask"

What moment do you
remember best from your
childhood summers?

Family
dinner table

Take a leisurely bike ride.

"Rain"

that I can then begin writing new material.

"The problem, however, is that I seldom know what I did wrong. I know it's wrong, but not where, what, why, how or when. Thus, I make changes and change them back . . . it can be a long process, but it always eventually works out."

ponder the book, or I begin
to edit the previously written
sections. I might go through
everything I've already written
a hundred times, tweaking and
changing little things, as if I'm
trying to find my way through
a darkened room. And little
by little, I find those errors.
Once they're corrected, I find

and *The Notebook*. "It's as if my mind tells me that I'm wrong somehow, and that I'd better stop because I'm heading in the wrong direction. Thus, I find myself writing more slowly until I simply can't write anymore—a classic case of writer's block. In a situation like that, I quit trying to press forward and instead

Expert Advice:

Nicholas Sparks, novelist

"When I'm blocked, it's nearly always because—sub-conscious-ly—I know I've made a mistake either with character development, structure, or story," confesses best-selling author Nicholas Sparks, whose novels include *A Walk to Remember*

...aspects of th...

...as design, cu...

...sions; quality co...

...ply ch... man...

...keting &...

...ed to b...

Hand write a letter
to someone you
haven't seen in
a long time.

Try to write without stopping.
Keep it going for five minutes.
If the urge strikes to string
words together, do so.

Write random words.
Just type.

If you are feeling anxiety,
do some deep breathing
in a comfortable place
before revisiting the task
at hand.

Don't panic.

Edit later, once you
have a long list.

Remove the filters on your initial brainstorming. Write down EVERY idea.

Where should a project start? The kernel of an idea usually doesn't arrive when you are sitting at the computer. It arrives while you are driving, while taking a shower, while dreaming, or while engaged in an important conversation having nothing to do with your creative life. Don't trust your memory. Write down ideas as quickly as possible.

"Reach"

Go to the library and find the most recent anthologies of *Best American Short Stories*, *Best American Essays* or similar collections with superlatives in their titles.

Read one story from
each collection.

Go to an expensive restaurant by yourself.

Take your time and people watch. Make at least one note about the people at every table.

Ask a librarian to tell you about
the most unusual request he or
she has gotten for information.

Imagine why that person would
be looking for that.

"Silence"

Expert Advice:
Robert Falls, theater director

Does a Tony-winning Broadway director ever stare at the actors and think, "I've got nothing"?

"All the time," admits Robert Falls, Artistic Director of Chicago's acclaimed Goodman Theatre and director of

Broadway's *Aida* and *Death of a Salesman*. "In the rehearsal room sometimes I keep talking even though I don't know what I'm going to come up with."

As director, Falls often has months to work on a play before bringing on actors and the rest of the creative crew. "Usually there

are a set of problems that I have
to struggle with anywhere from
three months to a year before
anyone comes in on it. Once you
bring in the collaborators, I tell
them what I'm struggling with
in hopes that someone else will
come up with an idea." When
he's aware of a problem but not

a solution, Falls often takes a step back. "What I try to do is plant the problem in the unconscious in hopes that the unconscious will solve it. If you sit there staring at it trying to solve it, you are often too conscious. It's like when you know that you know somebody's name

but you can't remember it.
You are better off not trying to
remember it.

"There was this moment in
Aida when a whole sequence
wasn't working. The solution
really did come to me in the
shower. Under the hot water
came a way to consolidate three

scenes wrapped around a song.

"I embrace a play or project *because* of its problems," says Falls. "Shakespeare's late plays are often called 'the problem plays' because they have high shift in tone and are often difficult to stage. I find them his most glorious plays."

Imagine a place that no person has seen before.

Save time at the end of
your writing day to print
out what you've written
and edit it on paper.

The next time you sit down to work, you'll have something to do besides wonder how you're going to get started. Without realizing it, you'll have started adding new material to your work.

"Luxury"

Go to an antique
shop and find an
unusual item.

Learn its history.

If you are working in a group, pair off and have each group tackle the problem for a predetermined period of time.

Come together.

Present.

Listen.

Argue.

Merge.

Try to remember every
Halloween costume
you've ever worn.

"Shopping spree"

What was the first job
you can remember
wanting to have?
Archeologist? Spy?
News anchor?

Research that job until
you find 10 things you
didn't know about it.
List those.

"Now there's something you don't see every day."

Get out of your own backyard.

Use glossy travel magazines to help you come up with new locations for your work.

Keep a journal.

Whenever you find yourself stuck for more than half an hour on your project, turn to your journal and start writing. Stop after 15 minutes and return to the task at hand.

"Wake up!"

"Spring"

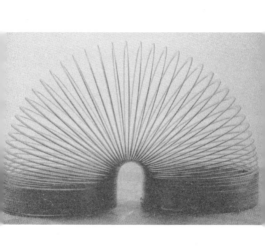

"Bottle"

Itemize the contents of your purse or wallet.

Under an overpass

Go to the supermarket.

Search for three items
you've never tasted
before. Try them.

"Slow"

Write about a woman
who can't remember
where she needs to be.

"Clean up this room."

Recall the last
time you raised
your voice.

Stretch.

Paul F. Tompkins, comedian

Paul F. Tompkins was a writer
and series regular on the land-
mark HBO series *Mr. Show*.
An acclaimed stand-up comic,
with HBO and Comedy Central
specials to his credit, he hosts
a weekly show at the L.A. Club
Largo.

"As far as my 'creative process' goes, this is all I can tell you: I need a deadline. I am extremely undisciplined as a writer and I need the fear to make me creative. I can come up with an idea any old time, but actually fleshing it out and completing it requires some sort of threat to be present. Working with other

people is different because
you're going back and forth,
and it doesn't feel like work,
but left to my own devices, I'll
put it off and put it off and put
it off. Then, as the deadline
approaches, the fear takes over.
And I'm usually happy with
the results.

"I like to say, it takes pressure to make a diamond."

Select some music without lyrics, put it on your stereo, and turn it up a little louder than you usually do. Lie on the floor and close your eyes.

Let your mind go
where it wants.

"Smooth"

What is the lamest gift
you ever gave?

What was the best?

Google an ex.

Create a cause and events chain. Write down a one-sentence action. Follow it by an action it causes, then an action that one causes. Continue the list until you find yourself compelled to write at greater length. Then remove the one-sentence limit.

Imagine a person facing
the moment of realization
that he or she is broke.

Scrub your bathroom.

You'll be amazed at how quickly you'll want to get back to creative work.

Remember how you used to
play games as a kid?
Remember the combination
of fierce competition and
easy distraction?

Think of your current
project as a game,
played with friends.

Cathedral

"Wash"

Ask the most interesting
person you know to have
dinner with you.

"Hey!"

Take a walk around
the block.

Invent a misunderstanding
that leads to an argument.

The scene of
an accident

"Stalk"

Open an encyclopedia
to a random page.

Read everything
on that page.

If your deadline isn't
urgent, see three movies
in a day. In between each
screening, write for
a half hour.

Apologize to someone.

Sometimes what is blocking you has nothing to do with the task at hand.

Read a Shakespeare
soliloquy out loud.

Take a serious shot
at understanding
its meaning.

"You can only choose one."

Fifty years ago, the year 2005 was the stuff of science fiction. Think about 50 years from now. What will be different? What will be the same?

"Endless"

Imagine a person who is moving cross-country. Come up with a story about the reasons for his move.

"Old-fashioned"

Listen to the complete
score of a Broadway show.

What's the longest you've ever gone in an average day without talking (not counting sleep time, of course)?

Think about the silences.

"Wish"

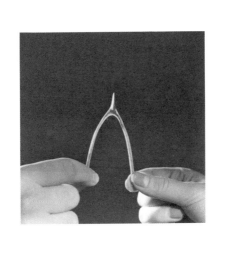

Often we place value in length. The epic novel and the three-hour movie seem more important than the poem or the sketch or other short form. There's a whole genre of short-short stories, though. And one of the most prestigious theater festivals, the Humana Festival for New American Plays, annually hosts a 10-minute play competition. Challenge yourself to create something very, very short.

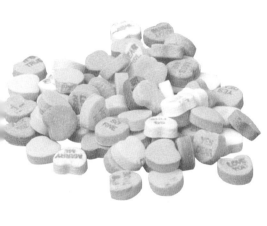

"Balance"

Cornelia Biddle—along with her husband Steve Zettler—pens the popular *Crossword Mysteries* series under the pseudonym Nero Blanc. No surprise: She likes to do word games.

"Steve was addicted first," she says. "I thought he was stupid to

waste his time with this, then I
became addicted because he
asked a question that was in the
L.A. Times crossword that he
couldn't get but I was brilliant
enough to know the answer.
They are addictive and they do
allow your mind to wander to

other places, especially if they are hard. I love the ones that send me to the encyclopedia."

Another trick: Tapping into their earlier lives as actors (Biddle was a regular on *One Life to Live*, her husband appeared

on Broadway in *A Soldier's Play*).
"We tend to act things out when
we get into a bind in terms of
dialogue."

Get up
and dance.

Go ahead. No one's looking.

Visual artists often
combat creative block
by switching media.

What are the tools that you are using? How can you replace them?
(It might be as easy as going from the keyboard to pen and paper.)

A city park at night.

Write about an ordinary
person who does
something heroic.

What is the first painting you remember seeing? Write down everything you can remember about it, including where you were and who you were with when you saw it.

Give yourself a confined, specific amount of time to create something new.

"Flat tire"

Identify your favorite shirt
or other article of clothing.
Write out its history and
why it has such positive
feelings for you.

Start a file or scrapbook
of photos, ads and other
images that inspire you.

Consult it whenever
you feel stuck.

Play a round of miniature golf.

"Search"

Recall the last loud argument you were a participant in. Imagine the scene from the point of view of a child witness.

"Nailed"

Play a game of Scrabble

Or Boggle.

It is estimated that more than 3.75 million people bowl in weekly leagues. Write about one of these people.

"Self-defense"

An unusual museum

Think about the last book you finished reading. No doubt there were sentences—even paragraphs, perhaps even chapters—that you skimmed.

Flip through the book again. Try to figure out what made you shift into speed-reading mode. Too much description? Excessive dialogue? A narrator telling you what you already knew?

Expert Advice: Frank Delaney, award-winning BBC journalist and bestselling author

The acclaimed Irish writer whose books include *The Celts* and *Ireland: A Novel* says, "The problem with most creative blocks is that they come from the very thing that fuels most creativity. That's depression. The best work comes out of being depressed. I invented a way out that has proven completely fruitful. It has never failed. I take down a book by one of my favorite writers—it could be someone from the past, an old childhood favorite, or someone who published a non-fiction book I enjoyed last year— and I copy several pages. Just type them out. That way, I find out how they did it. I find out

how human and fallible have
been these literary heroes. By
doing this, you realize that they
too had their struggles.

"I have a second tip as well.
When I'm faced with creative
block, I go and research something in relation to the book. In
the researching I deliberately let
go of that day's discipline a little

and allow myself to be diverted
by other engaging topics. If I'm
looking up something from 1951
in old newspapers, I allow myself
to go to another story and follow
it. And I'll do that for up to an
hour. When I come back, I'm
refreshed and invigorated and my
own subject has been stimulated."

Take a bath.

Listen to your favorite
songs from high school.

Read an out-of-town
newspaper. Ignore the
big world events that
are covered everywhere.

Focus on the local stories—the ones that are unlikely to impact your life but are significant to those in that region.

Your dilemma is not unlike that of a burglar trying to break into a house. You are trying one way to create your project, just as a burglar may try one way to break into a house. Bad creators—and bad burglars—give up at the first sign of resistance. There are lots of other windows.

Keep trying
until you find
the open one.

Doodle.

Don't be afraid to
let words work
their way in.

Some creative people work better under pressure. Even if you don't have one, try giving yourself a very formal deadline. Treat it as if there were monetary or other rewards involved.

Give meeting the deadline
a higher priority than
producing brilliant work.
You can edit later (under
another made-up deadline).

"Lost"

Write about one person
trying to convince another
to do something both
know is wrong.

A subway

Go to the library and find local newspapers from the weeks or months just before you moved to your hometown.

Explore the things that
we accidentally miss.

"Naked"

What scares you?

Bad web sites throw too much at you at once. They lead (or mislead) you on tangents, taking you places you didn't want to go. They distract you with unnecessary information. The same goes—usually less obviously—for bad books, plays and movies.

Take your project and look for places where clutter is getting in the way.

"Visitor"

Imagine an outdated object found at a thrift shop or garage sale.

Think about an issue
that you feel very
strongly about.

Now imagine the
circumstances that would
make you change your mind.

Write about a smell.

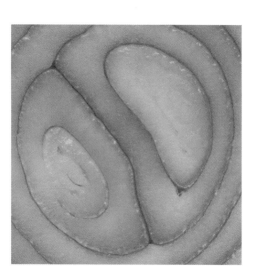

Recall a story that you were told which you didn't believe.

Now write it as if it really happened.

Plant something.

Read reviews. Don't pay too much attention to the reviewers' assessments of quality. Instead, note how quickly the plots and characters are summed up.

Write a review of
a project you have
yet to complete.

Make a list of the things
you know will definitely
be a part of your final
project—things like
length, materials, size, etc.

Knowing the things you
can't change enables you to
provide the foundation for
the things you can.

"Justice"

Run.

The beach
at night

Take some swings
in a batting cage.

List all of the things you bought on your last shopping trip.

Write a sentence
or two about
each one.

Give yourself a holiday.

If you've written every day for a long stretch, take a day off . . . but take a notebook with you.

Do an Internet search on any of the creative people featured on the Expert Advice pages of this book. Most have their own websites.

Ask yourself what
you would put on
your own personal
website.

"Trash"

Imagine something
inanimate coming
to life.

Imagine the consequences
of an unexpected piece
of mail.

Cut shapes out of
construction paper.

What piece do you
usually pick when
you play Monopoly?
The shoe? The race car?
The Scottie?

Write about
a full-sized
version of
that object.

"Hot"

The deck of a cruise ship

Ask your parents for help.

Seriously.

People are interested in conflict—
two forces opposing each other,
each wanting different things.
Make a list of a day's worth of
conflict, from the mundane to the
major.

"Escape"

Explain it:
Something is discovered
in the garden.

Solve a word-find puzzle.

Don't cheat.

Anna Grossnickle Hines,
children's book writer

"I don't really experience writer's block," says children's book author Anna Grossnickle Hines, author of such books as *Big Like Me* and *Daddy Makes the Best Spaghetti*, "but I do suffer from 'writer's avoidance.' I intend to

write. I want to write. But first
I'll get another cup of tea.
Maybe a snack. I'll just walk
out to see how the pond is
doing, or the flower garden.
Stop to deadhead a few. Water
a dry spot. I get myself to the
computer. But first I'll check
my email. Maybe I'll click on
the Hunger Site and the Child

Health Site, such worthy causes, and it only takes another minute to check to see how my ROTH funds are doing—usually a mistake. Then maybe a quick game of Solitaire, just one, or two, or . . .

"One trick to avoid getting into this loop is to get a story rolling in my head before I head

for the computer. My second
trick, very useful when there are
lots of other things that I really
do need to attend to—an illus-
tration deadline, for example—is
to set myself a time limit. I know
I don't have all day, but I'll 'let'
myself write for only 15 minutes
or an hour. No time to waste
now! I have to get going. And

the third thing, which I've heard many other writers say, is to write every day. It's so much easier to get started if I'm writing regularly and, going back to my first trick, I'm more likely to have that story rolling, to be playing it over in my head as I put in the load of laundry, or set the hose to water an area of lawn, or whatever tasks might otherwise be helping me avoid writing. Now the time spent doing those chores becomes part of my 'writing time.'"

Organize a poker game
with people who you
think are creative
thinkers.

Build in time for an
impromptu focus group
(warn them when you
extend the invitation).

Recall the moment in life when you felt most like a fish out of water.

Write about a bad
reason for giving
someone flowers.

A gathering for the big game

"Summer love"

Recall a memorable
school project.

"Let's try something different."

Talk to people who
answer questions as part
of their daily routine.

What do people ask a concierge? What's the first thing people ask the information desk when they get off a plane?

If your ideas have run out,
edit something you've
already written. Imagine
that you are reading
these words for the
first time.

Be very, very critical.

"America"

Much is written about pets we love. Write about you (or someone else) and a disliked pet.

Expert advice: David Gerrold, science fiction writer

"Okay, here's an easy exercise," offers David Gerrold, who has won just about every science-fiction writing award since first penning the classic *Star Trek* episode "The Trouble With Tribbles." "Sit down and write

a conversation between you
(the author) and your character.
   "Ask him what he wants,
what he needs, what's on his
mind. Ask where he came from,
how he feels about his family,
what happened in school,
how he got that scar, who's
the woman who hurt him, etc.

Let him answer from his experience. That's the first part. Second part, let the character quiz you. Why are you doing

this to me? Is there a way out?
How do I solve this problem?
And see how you answer.
   "Works every time."

Imagine a job you'd hate.

"Fortune"

A zoo

Imagine what goes on
in a person's head when
he or she leaves a job
or a home.

Make a list of everything you read in a given week.

What do these sources
of information and
entertainment say
about you?

Meditate or pray.

Treat this as a way to
clear or focus your mind
rather than as an act
of desperation.

Imagine where you will be tomorrow, next week, or whenever the project is complete. Accept that, at some point, it will be done.

Relax and move
forward with
that knowledge.

Remind yourself of 10 undesirable things you could be doing instead of creating.

When the ideas
start to flow,
minimize
distractions.

Take the phone off the hook.

Shut the door.

Reschedule appointments.

Keep rolling.

"End"

Photography Credits

ABOUT THE AUTHOR

Lou Harry's more than 20 books, as author or co-author, include *The Game of Life*, *The Encyclopedia of Guilty Pleasures*, *Portable Voodoo*, and *The High-Impact Infidelity Diet: A Novel*. Combined, they've sold more than a million copies. He has written hundreds of magazine articles and is currently editor in chief of *Indy Men's Magazine*. If you are stuck for an idea—or would like Lou to run a writers' workshop for you or speak to your group—contact him at workforlou@aol.com.